# The Stock Market Trading Cheat Code

**Mantras** that will never let you lose even a single dime

Time to cheat the **Operators** at their own game

JK Bull

Publishing Mongers

First Published in **June 2024**

**ISBN: 978-93-6356-091-8**

**PUBLISHING MONGERS**

**+91 9311101365**

**Distributed by:** Watergies

# Preface

How to play the operator.

# Foreword

This book is a way to navigate everyone that is out to get you. If you stick to what the author tells you, you will never lose. You will navigate all the traps and understand what it means to play the market.

# Acknowledgments

A heartfelt thanks to the publishing team for everything you have done for The Stock Market Trading Cheat Code.

# About the author

I could be someone who is speaking from experience, or I am someone who has learnt from the best, but I might be someone who is involved with the operators, and is somewhat tired of how they play you. I cannot say any more than that. Understanding the game is upto you. Take it or leave it.

# Dedication

This one is dedicated to everyone who has lost even a single cent in the market.

# Introduction

You are just a player, and someone else controls the game. They cheat, and you need to know the cheat code to survive. Stick to these Mantras in the market, and you will never fall for another one of those traps. This book will teach you the golden rules to never lose another dime. Think of a market where you can never lose anything, but again everything with the least bit of capital in your hand. Give it a try, and you will never look elsewhere. It is time you know The Stock Market Cheat Code

# Prologue

How many times have you made an investment where you were in green, but then you saw red ?

# Mantra no 1

You do not control the Market

Don't even for a second think that you have any sway over the market. You are a retailer, and while there are millions others like you, but you are not banded together. Institutional investors control the market, and they will do everything they can to take your money.

# Mantra no 2

## Don't wait on it

How many times have you made an investment where you were in green, but then you saw red. Don't wait for the red. Exit as soon as you see green, because it is not going to shoot up instantly. It is going to go up, then go down before it goes up again. Exit at the up to rejoin at the down. With this, you will be making more money than you would have made on holding it.

# Mantra no 3

## Risk Reward

Always evaluate your risk reward ratio. Let the reward be less, but the risk should be even lesser. Do not face a high risk with limited reward. That is your money at the end, earn as much as you can, but don't lose anything.

# Mantra no 4

## Find a Range

You need to find a range. Every instrument stays in a particular range on a particular day without any extraordinary events. Find the range, and repeatedly trade in that range.

# Mantra no 5

## Buy on the Dip

Never buy something on the top, because it has space to fall. Buy it always on the dip where the instrument has the space to rise.

# Mantra no 6

## Choose One

Don’t get involved with multiple instruments, choose one that suits you and understand it. Focus on it, know everything that is to know about it, and make money.

# Mantra no 7

## Beware of the Charts

The market operators know everyone is watching the charts. They are going to try their best to make a move against historical data, even if it is momentarily. Take a decision with your gut feeling, and you will never go wrong.

# Mantra no 8

## Holding Power

You should always be able to hold. When you get into a trade, you must have the power to hold it for a few days. In that case, if something goes wrong, you can ride out the bad time to enter into the good times.

# Mantra no 9

## Never play on Margin

Margin is attractive. It is to everyone. On a positive day, when you evaluate your situation, you cannot help but think I could have made at least five times what I made today. That is the age old trap. At that time, remember your bad days, when you could have lost five times of what you lost that day.

# Mantra no 10

## Firefight

As a rule, try entering a trade with about ten percent of your capital. Trade in and get out a safe profit. But, if the market does not favour you, deploy in the next ten percent and you will have ten opportunities for the same result.

# Mantra no 11

## Maintain your Target

When you are in firefight mode, don't sell the latest buy at a profit. But, maintain your target until you have used at least fifty percent of your capital. That will help you with your by average if you want to exit, or in the alternate case, if you have confidence in your first buy and want to hit the target, then the gain will be exponential.

# Mantra no 12

## Live to fight Another Dav

If you go for a margin, and things don't go in your direction even due to an artificial volatility, you are trapped. Always have enough to hold what you have called for, and cash out another day.

# Mantra no 13

## Imagine your Worst

Always imagine what will happen in the worst situation before you make a trade. What is the worst outcome, and how long can ride the worst. You need to be aware of it before you get into something, because one day you will see it coming for a minute. It won't last, but you will see it.

# Mantra no 14

## Never Panic

You can never panic, because this is not a game for the weak hearted. You need to maintain your position if you cannot improve it. But, as soon as you panic, you are out of the game.

# Mantra no 15

## Bound to Screw up

You are bound to make a mistake. You will make a mistake someday, and you will regret it too. But, you need to learn from it and move on. If you get caught up with that mistake, you are just going go deeper into the same hole.

# Mantra no 16

## Don't Overplay your Hand

Never ever get out of your comfort zone, because you might be sure of a direction, but the market just might not be ready to head there. It might eventually get there, but it can take its time. You need to be there for it.

# Mantra no 17

## Patience

You cannot get impatient. Things might work out for you, but they might not work out as soon as you expect them to. You need to be patient and let things happen as they are meant to be.

# Mantra no 18

## Never go Short

If you cannot make delivery, you are done. Shorts are really attractive especially when you have just made a gain, and are expecting a correction. But, the market might have just a little more momentum before it corrects itself. Don't make that mistake.

# Mantra no 19

## Expect the Unexpected

Why does anyone make a loss ? Because they did not expect that coming. You need to expect it, and be prepared for it just in case. You are in the game and everyone is playing it. Be prepared to lose a battle to win the war.

# Mantra no 20

## Capital doesn't Matter

Grow at a uniform pace, with whatever you have. Target small profits, but increase your frequency. Think of it as earning a single cent X number of times, X being your goal. How many times can you earn a cent in a day. Watch your instrument before you invest in it, and take out that cent per unit as many time as you can.

# Mantra no 21

## Carried Away

You cannot get carried away. Things might be working out all of a sudden, but keep your composure because one small slip-on change the whole game.

# Mantra no 22

## Experimentation

You have to experiment with your approach to find out which suits you the most until you land at one you believe in. While doing that, do not expose yourself. Always keep yourself covered.

# Mantra no 23

## One fits All

Does one move really suit everyone ? If you are scalping, maybe. But you have to find your one. Always know that your entry is someone else's exit. Question yourself, why ?

# Mantra no 24

## All or Nothing

All or nothing sounds cool when someone says it, but it is not what you want to dabble with. If you want all or nothing, go bet on a match where there are definitive results. Leave your gambler outside when you enter the market, because the markets eat up gamblers on a daily basis.

# Mantra no 25

## When

You always have to be sure about the when. Plan ahead. Before you make a buy, you have to know when you want to exit. The potential reward could be higher but the potential loss could be too. Always know and remember the when.

# Mantra no 26

## Know the Game

If you are going for a stock, you have to know what is the bottom, the least possible price that it can touch. When you get there, there is one single window of opportunity where you can never go wrong. Try to grasp it, and hold it as long as you want.

# Mantra no 27

## Fear

The market will scare you at every turn. That is the nature of the market. Quite often you are going to feel you made a blunder, and more often than not, it is a ploy. The market will scare you, but you have to be ready to fight.

# Mantra no 28

## How Long

How long you want to stick to these particular principles is upto you. It all depends on how long your goal is the same. But the crux of all this is to never lose anything. Earn more, earn less, but don't lose the more or the less.

# Mantra no 29

Wait

Wait to find the range. The markets move a little before they settle in a range. They will give you better returns in the movement, but they will take it too. If you have the capital to double down or even triple down, play the movement with your holding power. But don't put in everything on the movement. Wait for it. You will get your window.

# Mantra no 30

## Predefined Goal

You need to have a predefined goal you want to achieve, and you need to work towards it. At the end of the day, check how far you are and that will motivate you to trade better the next day.

# Mantra no 31

## Don't listen to Predictions

Do not listen to anyone's predictions, because it is not their money. Act with your own judgement, and you will never fail. It is your money, and it has to be your call.

# Mantra no 32

## Scalp

You need to scalp. You cannot keep waiting for a miraculous growth. You need to exit as soon as you are winning, because someone is already laying a trap to make you lose.

# Mantra no 33

## Economies of Scale

You know economies of scale is the best move, but what if you are not ready to play with all your capital. Does not matter. Start achieving the scale with a single unit. That is going to require harder work, but that will give you the same result.

# Mantra no 34

## Never Back Down

When you have made a call that does not have anything to do with the time value of the instrument, don't back down. No matter how much you regret your call today, you will break even. It might take its time, but it will get you there.

# Mantra no 35

## Never book a Loss

You are not playing at an institutional level. You do not have access to virtually unlimited funds. You are playing it small, and you need to get big. You cannot afford to lose even a single cent. You need to wait for it to go green, and then exit as per your will, but booking a loss is not an option. Don't play on margins, don't short and you will never book a loss.

# Mantra no 36

You make your own Game

Think of the entire market as whole universe in a game. You can play only one, and you need to excel at it. It is always better being a King of one rather than the Jack of all. There are stocks, futures, options, commodities, currencies, bonds and what not. Stick to one, preferably a single stock and work your way in it.

# Mantra no 37

## Take out your Capital

You cannot do this on day one, but soon you will have your capital safe, and a good profit to continue your pace. Take out your capital, and play with your profit. That makes your risk virtually zero, and will even allow you to trade better.

# Mantra no 38

## Sleep on It

If you have to make a decision which you are not satisfied with, do not take it in the heat of the moment. Sleep on it for a day, reevaluate everything, and then decide. You do not want regret eating at you.

# Mantra no 39

## The Good and the Bad

There will be good days, and there will be bad days. No matter how careful you are, there will be both. You need to balance them in order to succeed. Don't let either of them influence your decisions.

# Mantra no 40

## Don’t get Scammed

There will be a lot of attractive options to put your money in. If you see extraordinary returns, revaluate the whole thing before getting into it because everyone is laying out a trap for someone else, and you need to avoid it at all costs.

# Mantra no 41

## You are Alone

Once you go into the market, you are alone. Your family or friends cannot protect you or help you. You have to navigate alone, and you have got to win alone.

# Mantra no 42

## Zero Sum

This is a zero sum game where if you are winning, someone is losing. Always remember you are going against seasoned investors, and they will not fall for a trap you lay out, but they have enough experience to trap you. Avoid all these traps as much as you can. And if you get caught, fight for your survival.

# Mantra no 43

## Neither Bull nor Bear

Don’t play for the Bull side, don’t play for the Bear side. Play for you side, because it is only you who matters. Let the markets be bullish, let them be bearish, you just focus on your gain and nothing else will matter.

# Mantra no 44

## When to Enter

You should know when to enter, what is a comfortable price for the day, where the instrument is going to stay in. Once you find the entry point, you can enter and exit any number of times, walking out with a profit every time.

# Mantra no 45

## When to Exit

Don't wait for a range exit. If you see the instrument rise a little after you exit, it means you made the right call, because after this it is going to fall, and you do not want to ride the fall. Instead, you want to buy the fall.

# Mantra no 46

## The Jump before the Drop

Most of the times, an instrument is going to jump a little, just a little before it drops and changes range. Your exit should be in the jump range, and you will never fall with the drop.

# Mantra no 47

## Decision

Even with knowing all these tricks, the decision will be yours in the live market. No one can tell you the range. No one can tell you the entry. No one can tell you the exit. You will have to make the decisions based on your judgement.

# Mantra no 48

## Dynamics

The market is going to keep changing. If you have figured out a range in the morning, the instrument might change its range by the afternoon. You need to evolve with the range, and change your strategy accordingly.

# Mantra no 49

## History might not Work

What worked for you yesterday, or even until today might not work out any more. You need to change your approach with the change in the situation, but the basic principles remain the same.

# Mantra no 50

## Back Out

Back off when you achieve your goals. You need to reevaluate everything you have known, analyse your journey, conclude you future approach and start again. Keep what you have, and start afresh from time to time.

Target

Write your target here

Your personal strategy

Your personal Mantra

Write it down

You will need it soon

www.ingramcontent.com/pod-product-compliance
Lightning Source LLC
Chambersburg PA
CBHW080536250926
51846CB00016B/1307